The United States Government

by Etta Johnson

Table of Contents

Introduction

A national capital is the city where a country's government is based. Washington, D.C. is the capital of the United States.

This book will take you on a trip around Washington, D.C. You will see important places. You will learn about the three branches of the United States government.

bill

Constitution

democracy

executive branch

House of Representatives

judicial branch

justices

legislative branch

Senate

See the Glossary on page 30.

What Is a Democracy?

▲ The Constitution is in the National Archives Building on Constitution Avenue.

We will begin our trip on Constitution Avenue. It is named for the **Constitution** of the United States. The Constitution is the paper that tells about the U.S. government. It is a very important document. It describes the laws, rights, and beliefs that form the government.

The Constitution was written in 1787. You can still see it today in the National Archives in Washington, D.C.

The Constitution describes the U.S. government as a **democracy**. In a democracy, the citizens vote to choose their leaders. Citizens are people with rights in the country where they live.

Representatives are leaders chosen by citizens to say and do what is best for them. The Constitution describes how the representatives are chosen.

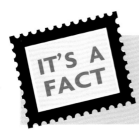

IT'S A FACT

U.S. citizens who are found guilty of serious crimes lose their right to vote.

▲ This is the Constitution of the United States. It gives citizens the right to vote.

Chapter 1

In a democracy, people have many rights. The U.S. Constitution has a part called the Bill of Rights. It was added to the Constitution in 1791. Here are some of the rights it describes.

▲ People can choose their religion.

▲ People can have meetings.

In a democracy, people can ask for changes in the government. The changes in the Constitution are called amendments. The first ten amendments are the Bill of Rights.

U.S. citizens can also ask the government to make changes. Citizens can write letters and make telephone calls. They can meet with their representatives in person.

◀ People can say what they think.

▲ These people are meeting with their representative. They see a problem in the government. They are asking the representative to help solve the problem.

In a democracy, no person or group in the government should have too much power. The people who wrote the Constitution knew this. They set up the government so that the power is divided. The power is divided among three branches of government.

The Constitution tells about the three branches of government. They are the legislative, the judicial, and the executive. Each branch has a different job to do. The branches check on each other.

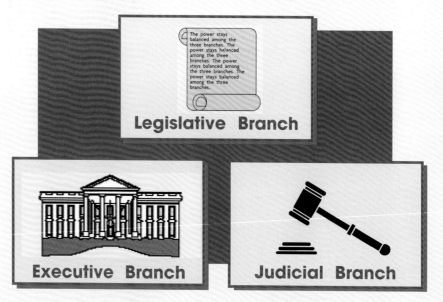

The Three Branches of Government

The power stays balanced among the three branches. The power stays balanced among the three branches. The power stays balanced among the three branches. The power stays balanced among the three branches.

Legislative Branch

Executive Branch

Judicial Branch

The **legislative branch** of government is called Congress. The legislative branch makes the laws.

▲ judicial branch   ▲ legislative branch

The **judicial branch** of government has judges and courts of law. The judicial branch solves problems with laws.

The first U.S. president was George Washington.

The **executive branch** of the government is led by the president. The executive branch helps to make laws. The executive branch makes sure the laws are followed.

9

What Does the Legislative Branch Do?

The next stop on our trip is the Capitol Building. This beautiful building was finished in 1829. Congress meets in the Capitol Building.

dome

north wing

Congress has two parts. One part is called the **House of Representatives.** The representatives meet in the south wing of the Capitol.

The other part of Congress is called the **Senate**. The senators meet in the north wing of the Capitol.

south wing

The House of Representatives has 435 members. Representatives come from every state. The number of representatives is based on the number of people in the state. For example, Wyoming has very few people. One House member represents the whole state. California, with many people, has 53 representatives.

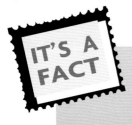

IT'S A FACT

Representatives must be at least 25 years old. They must have been U.S. citizens for at least seven years. They must live in the state they represent.

▲ Look for your state. How many representatives does it have?

Representatives meet to talk about laws. A **bill** is an idea for a new law. Representatives work in small groups called committees. Committees look at bills. A bill must be passed, or agreed upon, by both parts of Congress. Then the president must sign a bill before the bill can be a law.

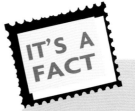

IT'S A FACT

The House has more than 20 committees. Examples are committees about health, energy, and education.

▲ Representatives talk about a bill in the House of Representatives.

13

▲ Senators talk about a bill
in the Senate.

The Senate has 100 senators. Each state sends two senators to Congress.

Senators work in committees to study bills, too. The Senate also approves people the president chooses for important government jobs.

MATH CONNECTION

Solve This

How many members of Congress are there altogether?

Answer: 535

The Senate is one part of Congress. The House of Representatives is the other part of Congress.

The House of Representatives has a leader. The leader is called the Speaker of the House. The Senate has a leader. The Vice President of the United States is the leader of the Senate.

▲ The vice president is the leader of the Senate.

IT'S A FACT

Senators must be at least 30 years old. They must have been a U.S. citizen for at least nine years, and they must live in the state they represent.

Who are your senators? Who is the representative from your part of the state? Make a chart like this one.

Congress

My Senator _____

My Senator _____

My Representative _____

Did You Know?

A political party is a group of people who share the same ideas about laws and government. There are two major political parties in the U.S., the Republican Party and the Democratic Party.

What Does the Judicial Branch Do?

The next stop on our trip is not far from the Capitol. It is the Supreme Court Building. This is the home of the judicial branch of the United States government.

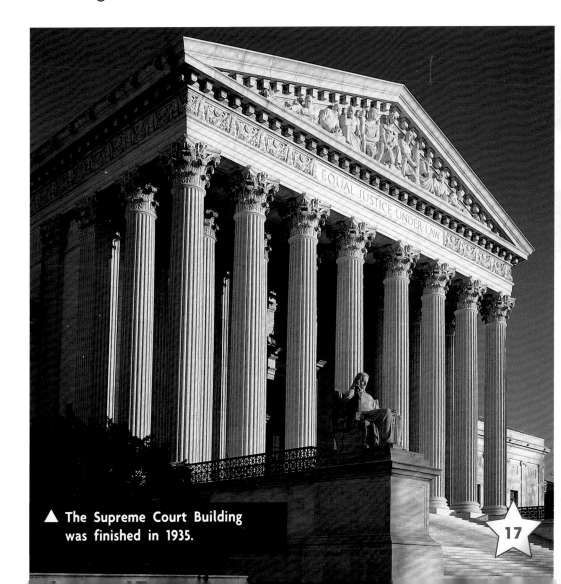

▲ The Supreme Court Building was finished in 1935.

The Supreme Court is the most important court in the United States. Nine judges, or **justices**, are on the Supreme Court. The leader of the justices is the chief justice.

When a new justice is needed, the president chooses someone. The Senate must approve that person.

The justices listen to important cases, or problems about the law. They listen to many people talk about the cases.

▼ **There are nine Supreme Court justices.**

The justices talk to one another. Then each justice thinks about his or her decision. They want to make sure the Constitution is followed. Finally, the justices vote on the case.

IT'S A FACT

At first the Supreme Court met in New York. Then it met in Philadelphia. Finally, it moved to Washington, D.C.

Other courts throughout the United States are part of the judicial branch. Courts protect people's rights. People are innocent until the courts decide they are guilty.

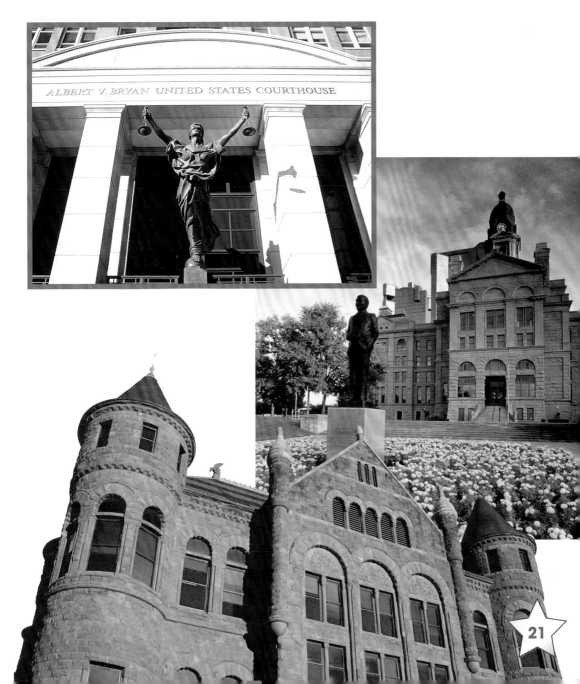

What Does the Executive Branch Do?

The next stop on our trip is the White House. The president lives and works here. The president leads the executive branch.

Leaders from all over the world visit the White House. They come for important meetings. They also come for dinners, dances, and parties.

The White House is in Washington, D.C. ▼

IT'S A FACT

The White House has 6 floors. It has 132 rooms and 35 bathrooms. It has 8 staircases and 3 elevators. It has 28 fireplaces.

The president has many jobs.

- The president works with Congress on laws.

- The president can suggest bills to Congress.

- The president can veto, or refuse to sign, a bill. If the president signs a bill, it becomes a law.

- The president leads the military.

- The president chooses people for important government jobs.

- The president meets with the leaders of other countries.

▲ The president meets with advisers every week.

The president works closely with people he trusts. These people are called advisers. They help the president with important decisions. Look at the list of departments on the next page. The leader of each department is an adviser to the president.

The executive branch must apply and enforce laws. The U.S. government has fifteen departments to do this. Many people work in each department.

The United States Government Departments

Department	Responsibility
Agriculture	farmers and food
Commerce	business and jobs
Defense	armed forces (army, navy, marines, air force)
Education	schools and universities
Energy	natural resources
Health and Human Services	health and medicine
Homeland Security	counterterrorism
Housing and Urban Development	homes and communities
Interior	national parks and land
Justice	U.S. laws
Labor	workers
State	other countries
Transportation	highways, railroads, airlines
Treasury	money and taxes
Veteran Affairs	people who served in the armed forces

A president is elected every four years. Citizens can vote for the president. Every citizen's vote counts.

▲ Election Day is an exciting time.

Presidents must be at least 35 years old. Presidents must have been born in the United States. They must have lived in the United States for at least 14 years.

We have three more stops on our visit. These places honor three important presidents.

The Washington Monument remembers the first United States president, George Washington.

The Jefferson Memorial remembers the third president of the United States, Thomas Jefferson. He wrote the Declaration of Independence.

The Lincoln Memorial remembers the sixteenth president of the United States, Abraham Lincoln. He worked to keep the country united.

27

The United States government has three branches.

United States Government

Legislative Branch

Judicial Branch

Executive Branch

Think About It

1. What does the legislative branch do?
2. What does the judicial branch do?
3. What does the executive branch do?

28

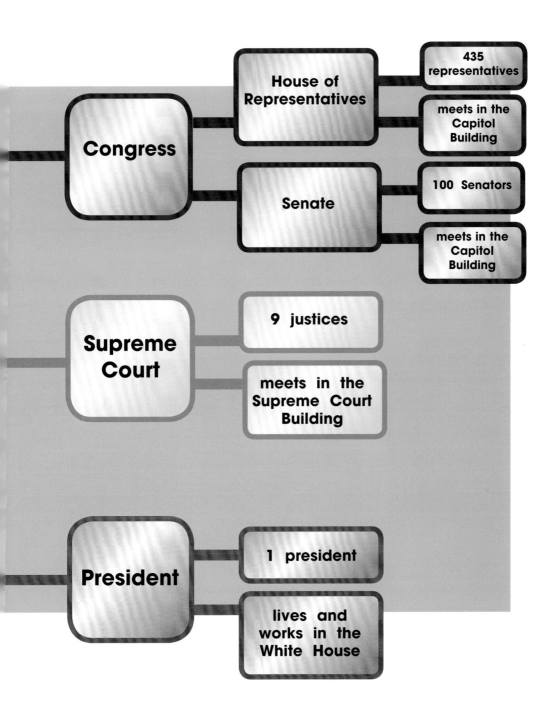

Congress

- **House of Representatives**
  - 435 representatives
  - meets in the Capitol Building
- **Senate**
  - 100 Senators
  - meets in the Capitol Building

Supreme Court

- 9 justices
- meets in the Supreme Court Building

President

- 1 president
- lives and works in the White House

bill an idea for a new law

*A **bill** does not always become a law.*

Constitution the document describing the laws, rights, and beliefs that form the U.S. government

*The United States **Constitution** was written in 1787.*

democracy a form of government in which people elect their leaders

*The United States is a **democracy**.*

executive branch the part of government led by the president that helps to make laws and makes sure they are followed

*The president leads the **executive branch**.*

House of Representatives the part of Congress made up of 435 representatives

*The **House of Representatives** meets in Washington, D.C.*

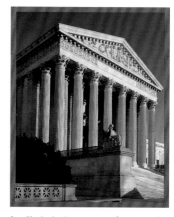

judicial branch the part of government that has judges and courts of law

*The **judicial branch** solves problems with laws.*

justices the judges on the Supreme Court

The justices listen to important cases, or problems about the law.

legislative branch the part of government that makes laws

The legislative branch has more than 500 members.

Senate the part of Congress made up of 100 senators

The Senate meets in Washington, D.C.

Index